Bible Stories
for Little Ones

A Frances Hook Picture Book

Standard® PUBLISHING

Cincinnati, Ohio

Published by Standard Publishing, Cincinnati, Ohio

www.standardpub.com

Copyright © 2011 by Standard Publishing

Printed in Hong Kong

Project editor: Karen Cain

Cover design: Andrew Quach

Illustrations by Frances Hook

Stories by Wanda Hayes and Karen Cain

ISBN 978-0-7847-3520-6

Library of Congress Cataloging-in-Publication Data

Hook, Frances.
Bible stories for little ones : a Frances Hook picture book / [illustrations by Frances Hook ; stories by Wanda Hayes and Karen Cain].
p. cm.
ISBN 978-0-7847-3520-6
I. Hayes, Wanda. II. Cain, Karen. III. Title.
BS551.3.H66 2012
220.9'505--dc23
2011051046

17 16 15 14 13 12   1 2 3 4 5 6 7 8 9

Contents

Noah and the Ark

Many, many years ago God spoke to a good man named Noah. He said, "Noah, I want you and your three sons to build a big boat called an ark. A great flood is coming, and I want you to be safe. This boat will protect you and your family."

Noah obeyed God. He and his sons built an ark, just as God said. When it was finished, God said, "Take two of every kind of animal and bird into the ark; take enough food for your family and for the animals." Noah did just what God said.

When Noah and his family and all the animals were inside the ark, God closed the door. Soon Noah and his family heard, "Pitter patter, pitter patter." It was the sound of rain, and it grew louder and louder. It rained and it rained. It rained for forty days and forty nights. But Noah and his family and all the animals in the ark were safe and dry.

After the rain stopped, the ark rested on top of a mountain. When the land was dry again, Noah and his family came out of the ark. All of the animals and birds came outside too. Noah prayed, "Thank you, God, for taking care of us."

—From Genesis 6:13–8:22

Jacob and Esau

Isaac and Rebekah were very happy. God gave them two strong baby boys. They were twins. One was named Esau and the other one was named Jacob.

God told Rebekah, "Your sons will be the leaders of two big groups of people someday."

Rebekah took good care of the sons God had given to her and Isaac. She taught them to love and obey God.

Jacob was a very quiet boy who liked to stay close to home and take care of sheep.

Esau liked to go into the fields and hunt animals for food, as his father did.

Isaac and Rebekah watched their young boys grow. Jacob and Esau were very different from each other, and many times the two brothers did not get along.

But when Jacob and Esau grew up and became men, they settled their differences and decided not to argue any more. God gave Esau a large family to lead. And God chose Jacob to be the leader of his special people, the Israelites.

—*From Genesis 25–36*

Baby Moses

Long ago a kind mother carried a little basket bed she had made for her baby boy. The mother and her daughter walked to the river with the baby in the basket bed. She was hiding her sweet little boy so the wicked king would not kill him.

"Shhh! Do not cry," the mother said to the baby as she kissed him. "Go to sleep. God will take care of you." Then she set the basket bed in the water to float among the tall grass. "Miriam, stay close and watch your baby brother," the mother said to her daughter.

The baby's mother left, and Miriam watched the little basket bed very closely. Soon a princess came to the river. "What do I hear?" she said. "It sounds like a baby crying." The princess looked and saw the basket bed. She saw the precious little baby boy. "I will not let the king hurt you," the princess said.

Miriam said, "I know someone who will take care of the baby for you."

"Go and bring her," said the princess.

Do you know whom Miriam brought to take care of her brother? It was their own mother! She must have thanked God very much for letting this princess find her baby.

The princess said, "I will name the baby Moses."

And Moses grew up to do wonderful things for God.

—From Exodus 2:1-10; Hebrews 11:23-29

Ruth and Naomi

"**G**oodbye, Ruth," Naomi said sadly. "I have to go back to the city where I used to live. You should go to your city too."

"No," said Ruth. "You are my dear friend, and I will not leave you alone. I will go with you. Your friends will be my friends. I will love and obey God as you do. I will be your friend for as long as you live."

So Naomi and Ruth, two women who loved God and each other, walked together to Bethlehem. Naomi's friends were very surprised to see her again, and even more surprised to see Ruth there too. But Ruth had made a promise to care for Naomi, and she planned to keep it.

When they needed food, Ruth went to a field where the men gathered tall, yellow grain. Sometimes they left a little grain on the ground. Ruth picked up the leftover grain and took it home to Naomi. Naomi used the grain to make bread for them to eat.

Ruth and Naomi said, "Thank you, God, for taking care of us." And Naomi probably prayed, "Thank you, God, for my dear friend, Ruth."

—From Ruth 1, 2

Hannah's Baby Boy

Hannah wanted a baby boy more than anything else in the world. So when Hannah and her husband went to worship God, Hannah kneeled and prayed. She said, "God in heaven, please give me a baby boy. I promise to take care of him and teach him to love you. He will work for you all his life."

Hannah and her husband went home. One day God gave Hannah a little baby boy, just as she had wanted. Hannah was very happy. She said, "I will name the baby Samuel."

Hannah loved Samuel very much and took good care of him. She fed him and washed him and put clean clothes on him. And, as all babies do, Samuel began to grow.

When Samuel was a little boy, his mother dressed him in his best clothes and took him back to the place where she worshipped God. Hannah went there to keep the promise she had made to God. She said to Eli, the man who lived there, "This is Samuel, the boy I prayed for. God gave him to me, and now I am giving him back to God, just as I said I would. Please take care of him and teach him how to love and serve God."

And Eli did take care of Samuel. Samuel stayed with Eli and became a good helper for God.

—From 1 Samuel 1

Samuel Hears God

Samuel liked learning about God. He liked helping his friend Eli. He liked staying in the place where people came to worship God. There was a lot of work to do there, and Samuel was a good worker.

Perhaps Samuel opened the big doors in the morning so people could come in. Maybe he helped sweep the floors and dust the furniture. Samuel probably did whatever Eli asked him to do. There were many ways a boy like Samuel could help.

One night after Samuel had gone to bed, he heard a voice call, "Samuel."

Who could it be? Samuel sat up in bed and looked around. But he didn't see anyone. "It must be Eli," he thought. So Samuel called out, "Here I am!" And he ran to Eli's room.

But Eli said, "I did not call you, Samuel. Go back to bed."

Again the voice called, "Samuel."

Samuel hurried to Eli and said, "I heard you call me." But Eli said, "I did not call you, my son. Go back to bed."

And the voice called Samuel again. But this time Eli told Samuel, "Go back to bed, and when you hear the voice again, say, 'Speak, Lord; I'm listening.'"

Soon Samuel learned that it was God's voice calling him. God had a special message to tell his good helper, Samuel. And this time, Samuel was ready to listen.

—From 1 Samuel 3:1-10

David the Shepherd

avid was a shepherd boy. He took care of his father's sheep. He led the sheep and the little lambs to big fields where they ate all the green grass they wanted. And when the sheep were thirsty, David took them to a stream of cool water to get a drink. He protected the sheep from lions and bears, and he cared about each sheep very much.

Sometimes David made up songs and sang them to his sheep. David sang many songs about God. When David thought about God, he felt just like a sheep; and God was the shepherd who took care of him. David wrote this song about God:

God is my shepherd; I have everything I need.
He leads me in green fields and by still waters.
He makes me strong.
He teaches me to do what is right.
I will not be afraid of bad things because I know
     God is with me.
I am very happy.
God will be good and kind to me all my life,
And I will live with him forever.

—From 1 Samuel 17:34, 35; Psalm 23

David the King

David took care of his father's sheep near the town of Bethlehem. David obeyed his father, and he obeyed his heavenly Father, God.

Just as David took care of the sheep, God took care of David. When a lion took one of David's sheep, David went after the lion and killed it. He brought the sheep safely back home to the other sheep. God helped David kill the lion. When a bear took one of David's sheep, God helped David kill the bear.

One time while David was watching his sheep, someone came running toward him calling, "David, David, hurry back home. A man has come to visit your father, and he wants to see you."

When David got to his house, he met the man who was asking for him. The man was Samuel, who had served God since he was a boy. Now Samuel was an old man. God had sent Samuel to find the next king for his people. And David, the shepherd boy, was the one God had chosen.

"When you grow up, you will be the king," Samuel told David.

God was pleased with David. David was a good shepherd boy, and God knew he would be a good king.

—From 1 Samuel 16:1-13; 17:34-37

A Room for Elisha

Elisha walked through many towns telling people how to live the way God wanted. Everyone who saw Elisha knew that he was a good man.

One day when Elisha came by a house, the woman who lived there said, "Hello, Elisha. Come and eat with my husband and me. We are glad to share our food with you. Come and rest in our house. You must be tired."

So Elisha ate with the man and woman. And every time Elisha walked through that town, he ate with them.

One day the woman said to her husband, "Elisha is one of God's helpers. Let's help him by building a little room for him. We can put a bed, a table, a chair, and a lamp in the room. Then Elisha will have a nice place to stay when he comes here again."

The next time Elisha visited the man and woman, they probably said, "Elisha, we have a surprise for you. We have built you your own room with a bed, a table, a chair, and a lamp. We want you to use this room because you are God's helper."

And every time Elisha visited the man and woman, he stayed in his own nice room. And perhaps Elisha prayed, "Thank you, God, for my kind friends and for this room."

—From 2 Kings 4:8-11

Naaman's Servant

Naaman was the captain of an army of the king. He was a great man, but Naaman was very sick. He had a disease on his skin, and no one could make him well. Naaman was sad and didn't know what to do.

A young servant girl who helped Naaman's wife said, "I wish that Naaman could visit God's helper, Elisha, in my country. He would make Naaman well."

When Naaman heard what the little girl said, he decided to go see Elisha and find out if he could make him well. So Naaman traveled to the land where Elisha lived.

When Elisha heard that Naaman was in his country, he sent someone to tell Naaman, "Go and wash seven times in the Jordan River, and you will be well."

Naaman went to the Jordan River and washed—one time—two times—three times—four times—five times—six times—seven times. When Naaman came out of the water the seventh time, he was well. His skin was clean and healthy! Naaman could hardly believe it. He was so happy he went back to Elisha and said, "Now I know that there is only one God. God made me well."

Naaman was glad that God made him well, and he was thankful for the little girl who helped him.

—From 2 Kings 5:1-15

Daniel Prays to God

Daniel prayed to God every morning, every afternoon, and every night. Daniel thanked God for many things. Daniel loved to talk to God.

In the country where Daniel lived, only a few people prayed to God. Some of the people did not like Daniel. They asked the king to make a law saying that anyone who prayed to God would be put into a den full of hungry lions.

But Daniel was not afraid. Every day he prayed three times in front of the window, where everyone could see him. Daniel thanked God just as he always did.

When the king found out, he had to put Daniel in the lions' den. But the king was Daniel's friend. He did not want Daniel to be hurt. The king was sorry he had made the law. He was sorry that his friend Daniel was in danger.

After Daniel had been in the lions' den all night, the king hurried there and called out, "Daniel, are you all right? Did your God take care of you?"

"Yes," said Daniel. "I am fine. God sent an angel to shut the lions' mouths. They did not hurt me."

Then the king let Daniel go back to his house. Every day Daniel knelt in front of the window and prayed three times to God, just as he always did. And no one ever bothered Daniel again for praying, because they knew how powerful and strong his God is.

—From Daniel 6

Jesus Is Born

God sent an angel to tell Mary and Joseph that they would have a baby. But this was no ordinary baby. This baby was God's Son, Jesus!

Mary and Joseph loved each other very much. And they loved God even more! As the baby inside Mary grew and grew, Mary and Joseph loved that baby too.

Mary and Joseph took a trip to the city of Bethlehem. While they were there, it was time for the baby to be born. But the city was so crowded that Mary and Joseph couldn't find anywhere to stay. All the rooms in all the buildings were already filled. So Mary and Joseph had to stay outside in the place where people kept their animals.

There were probably sheep and cows and donkeys and horses staying there with them. It probably didn't look very nice. It probably didn't smell very nice. But it was warm and dry, and they were together.

That night, the baby was born. He was God's Son, and his name was Jesus. Mary and Joseph wrapped the baby up so he would be warm, and they made a soft bed for him in the hay where the animals ate.

—From Matthew 1:18-21; Luke 1:26-38, 2:1-7

Happy Shepherds

On a grassy hillside one dark night, some shepherds were taking care of sheep. They watched the sheep very closely. They did not want the sheep to get lost. They did not want a hungry wild animal to hurt the sheep.

Suddenly there was a shining angel standing by the shepherds. They were so afraid.

"Don't be afraid," said the angel. "I have good news to make everybody in the world happy. Tonight in Bethlehem Jesus has been born. You will find him wrapped in soft clothes and lying in a manger."

Then suddenly there were many, many angels lighting up the dark sky. They said a special thank-you to God because Jesus was born.

When the angels were gone, the shepherds weren't afraid anymore. "Let's go see the baby the angel told us about." And they hurried as fast as they could.

The shepherds found the baby Jesus in a manger, just as the angel had said. They were so happy. They thanked God for his wonderful gift of Jesus.

—From Luke 2:8-20

A Special Baby

Mary picked up Jesus from the bed where he had been sleeping. She wrapped him in new, clean clothes. Today was a special day for their family. Today Joseph and Mary would take baby Jesus for a visit. They would take him to the temple, the place where people came to pray and worship God.

The temple was shiny and clean. It was almost like a church building. In one part some people were praying. In another part some people were singing to God.

A man named Simeon was at the temple. He knew Jesus was a special baby. Simeon held Jesus in his arms and praised God. A woman named Anna was also at the temple. She knew Jesus was a special baby too, and she told everyone there that Jesus was God's Son.

God knew Mary and Joseph would take good care of his Son, Jesus. And they did! Jesus grew taller and stronger and wiser every day.

—From Luke 2:22-40

A Woman by a Well

After Jesus grew to be a man, he traveled all around the country, teaching people about his Father, God. Jesus' friends went with him. They walked along the hot, dusty roads together.

One day when Jesus and his friends had walked for a long time, they stopped at a well to rest. A well is a deep, dark hole with cool water inside. A drink from the well sounded good to the hot, tired travelers.

While Jesus was at the well, a woman came to fill her pitcher. Jesus was thirsty. He said to the woman, "Would you please give me a drink?"

The woman was surprised. "Why do you speak to me—someone you don't even know?" she asked.

"If you knew who I am, you would have asked me for something," Jesus said, "something much better than a drink of water."

Jesus and the woman talked for a long time. Jesus told the woman many things about herself. All the time Jesus was talking, the woman may have been thinking, "I know this man is someone special. But who?" Then the woman said to Jesus, "I know that God promised to send Jesus, who will tell us everything."

Jesus must have looked at the woman very kindly as he said, "I am Jesus."

The woman was surprised and happy, all at once. She found something better than water. She found Jesus, the Son of God.

—From John 4:5-26

Jesus Heals a Sick Boy

One day a rich man who worked for a king came to Jesus and said, "My son is sick in another city. Please come and make him well. He is so sick that his mother and I are afraid he will die."

Jesus knew that the rich man believed he could make his son well. So Jesus told the man, "Go home. Your son is not sick anymore."

The rich man believed Jesus. He hurried back to his own city as fast as he could. And before he even got to his house, his servants came out to him and said, "Your son is alive. He isn't sick anymore! Come and see!"

The rich man knew Jesus had made his son well. And everyone in his house knew it too! They all believed that Jesus is God's Son.

Now the little boy could run and play again. He could hug his father and mother. He could do everything he used to do. The rich man and his wife and little boy were very happy. They were very thankful for Jesus.

—From John 4:46-54

Jesus Prays

Jesus loved to talk to God. Jesus talked to God just like we do, by praying. Even though God already knows everything we need, he wants us to pray.

One day, Jesus was teaching a large crowd. He taught about many important things. Jesus knew that talking to God was important, and so he showed his friends how to pray like this:

> Our Father in heaven,
> Your name is holy and great.
> Be our king here on earth,
> Just as you are in heaven.
> Please give us what we need for today.
> Forgive us for the wrong things we do,
> And help us forgive others when they do wrong.
> Help us stay away from bad things.
> Everything is yours, powerful God, forever.
> Amen.

—From Matthew 6:9-13

A Boy Gives His Lunch

Wherever Jesus went, crowds of people followed him. Some came to hear him tell about God and about how they should live. Sick people came to Jesus so he would make them well. Everyone wanted to be around Jesus.

One day a big crowd of people listened to Jesus nearly all day. They wanted to stay with Jesus so much that they didn't even go home to eat. Jesus knew the people were hungry so he asked his friends, "Where can we buy bread for these people?"

Philip said, "We do not have enough money to buy even one bite of bread for all of these people."

Then Andrew said, "There is a boy here who has five loaves of bread and two fish. But they will not feed everyone."

Jesus told everyone to sit down on the soft grass. Then he took the bread and fish the boy gave to him. Jesus prayed and thanked God for the boy's lunch.

Then something very special happened. Jesus gave his friends the bread and fish, and asked them to give it to all the people. Instead of five loaves and two fish, there was more and more! There was enough for everyone. There were even twelve baskets full of leftover food after everyone had eaten.

The crowds of people knew that only God could make so much food from one boy's lunch. God used one small gift to help thousands of people that day. They were grateful for Jesus and for one little boy who was willing to share.

—From John 6:1-13

The Kind Shepherd

One day Jesus told this story: "There was a shepherd who took care of one hundred sheep. Early in the morning he led them out of their safe pen and into the fields.

"The shepherd loved to walk with his sheep through the fields where they could eat soft, green grass. He loved to sit by a cool stream of water where the sheep could get a drink. The shepherd loved all his sheep very, very much.

"When the day was almost over, the shepherd took his sheep back home to their pen. As they went in the gate, he counted them, 'One, two, three, . . .' all the way up to ninety-nine. That's all there were. One sheep was gone.

"The kind shepherd closed the gate and went to find his lost sheep. He looked in the big grassy field. He looked by the stream. He climbed up the rocky hillside. He looked everywhere for the little lost sheep. 'I'm coming,' he called.

"Soon the shepherd found the poor, scared sheep. He lifted him very carefully up onto his shoulder. 'It's all right, little one. I will take you back home now.'

"The sheep was very happy, but the shepherd was happiest of all. Now all his sheep were home where they belonged, safe and sound."

—*From Luke 15:3-6*

A Son Comes Home

Jesus wants us to know how much God loves us, and so he told a story: "Once there was a father who had two sons. He loved both of his sons very much. But one son was not happy. He wanted to leave his father's house and move far away.

"This son said to his father, 'Part of everything you have is mine. Give me my share now and let me leave.' The father was very sad, but he gave the son what he wanted. The son left home and didn't look back. At first he was happy. He did whatever he wanted. But soon he had spent all his money and had nothing left. He didn't have a place to stay or money to buy food. He was alone and afraid and very, very homesick. He knew he had made a terrible mistake.

"The son decided to go back home and ask his father for a job. At least then he would have a place to stay and food to eat. He walked home slowly, worried that his father would be angry with him for leaving. He knew he had hurt his father very much.

"But the father wasn't angry at all. In fact, he was watching for his son, waiting for him to come home. He missed him terribly. When the father saw his son in the distance, he ran as fast as he could to meet him. He hugged him and kissed him and loved him as much as he ever did. They had a huge celebration because the son who left had come home."

—From Luke 15:11-24

A Man Thanks Jesus

Wherever Jesus went, people asked, "Please make me well." And Jesus did. He made people see again. He made people walk again. He made dead people come back to life again. The people knew that only God's Son could do these amazing things.

One day as Jesus and his friends started to go into a city, they heard some men call, "Jesus, teacher, help us." Jesus saw ten men who were very sick. They had bad sores on their bodies.

Jesus told them, "Go, show yourselves to the priests." The men did what Jesus said, and as they started to walk away they looked at their bodies. Their sores were all gone! Jesus made all ten men well. They were so happy.

Nine of the men hurried on into the city to show their friends and families that they were well. But one man came running back to Jesus. He got down on the ground at Jesus' feet and said, "Thank you, Jesus. Thank you for making me well."

Jesus wondered why none of the other men came back to say, "thank you." But he was very glad that one man did. Jesus knew this man really loved him.

—From Luke 17:11-19

Jesus and the Children

Jesus was sitting on a large stone. He saw the mothers bringing their little babies to him. He saw other boys and girls coming to him too. Some were tall; some were short. Some were big; some were little. Jesus loved them all, just as they were.

But Jesus' friends stood in front of him and frowned. They said, "Go back to your mothers, children. Jesus is very busy and doesn't have time for you right now. Go on now. Leave him alone."

Jesus stopped his friends and said, "Let the children come to me. I want to see them."

And the children ran to Jesus. Maybe they even climbed up in his lap. Jesus smiled warmly and patted each little child on the head. Perhaps he put his arms around the children as he talked to them. Then Jesus asked God to bless every boy and every girl.

All the children loved Jesus. And Jesus loved them too.

—From Matthew 19:13-15 and Mark 10:13-16

Jesus and Zacchaeus

"Jesus is coming! The Master is coming." All the people in town were talking about Jesus. They were excited that he would soon be in their city. Men and women, boys and girls crowded along the street to see Jesus.

"I want to see Jesus too," thought Zacchaeus. "But all of these tall people are in front of me, and I won't be able to see over their heads." Zacchaeus was a very short man. "I have heard so many wonderful things about Jesus," said Zacchaeus. "I have to see him."

Zacchaeus looked around, and then he had an idea. "I know how I can see Jesus!" And he climbed a tall tree by the street.

Zacchaeus looked out from the tree. Several men were coming down the street. One of them was Jesus! Soon Jesus would walk right under the tree where Zacchaeus was. But when Jesus got close, he didn't walk by the tree. Instead Jesus stopped underneath it, and looked up at Zacchaeus. Jesus said, "Zacchaeus, hurry and come down from there, because I'm going to stay at your house today."

Zacchaeus couldn't believe his ears! He did hurry down from the tree, and Jesus did stay at his house. Zacchaeus changed his whole life that day, all because of Jesus. Zacchaeus was very glad he climbed that tree.

—*From Luke 19:1-10*

A Song for Jesus

It was a special day in Jerusalem. Jesus was coming to worship God along with all the other people who were gathered in the city. When everyone heard that Jesus was coming, they went out to meet him. They spread their coats down on the road. These made a special carpet for Jesus—just like a king. Some of the people cut branches from trees and laid them in the road for Jesus.

Then Jesus came riding on a donkey. There were many, many people. They were so glad that they shouted, "Hosanna to the Son of David! Hosanna in the highest!" This was how they showed Jesus they loved him. This was their way of saying, "We know you are very special and very great."

Jesus got off the donkey and walked into the place where people worshipped God. Many sick people came to him, and Jesus made them well. And all the time he was there, Jesus heard the children singing to him, "Hosanna to the Son of David! Hosanna!" The children knew Jesus was their friend. They liked to sing to Jesus, and their songs made him glad.

—From Matthew 21:6-11, 14-16

A Lesson from Jesus

Jesus and his friends were eating dinner together. When they were finished, Jesus did something his friends had never seen him do before. He took a towel and a pitcher and poured clean water into a bowl. Jesus' friends watched everything that he did.

"What is he doing?" they may have wondered. Soon they knew.

Jesus began to wash their feet with the water and dry them with the towel. Their feet were very hot and dirty from walking along the dusty roads. The cool water felt good. But they didn't understand what Jesus was doing.

When Jesus washed Peter's feet, Peter asked, "Why are you washing my feet?" Peter didn't think Jesus should do a dirty job like that because Jesus was God's Son.

After Jesus washed the feet of all his friends, he sat down again and answered Peter's question. "I have washed your feet to teach you to do kind things for each other and for other people."

Jesus' friends did as he asked. They were kind to each other. They were kind to other people too. And they always remembered the time when the mighty Son of God kneeled down and washed their dirty feet.

—From John 13:3-17

Jesus Is Alive

Many people loved Jesus. But many other people hated him. They didn't want to listen to him anymore. They didn't believe that he was God's Son. And so they decided to get rid of Jesus.

It was nighttime, and Jesus was praying in a garden. Jesus knew that he would die, and that it was part of God's plan. Jesus would pay for all the wrong things anyone had ever done or ever would do. While he was praying, soldiers came to the garden and took Jesus away. They nailed Jesus to a cross, and he died. It was a sad, sad day for Jesus' friends. They didn't understand that it was part of God's plan, and that God wasn't finished yet.

Jesus' friends took his body down from the cross and put it in a tomb. A huge stone was rolled in front of the doorway so that no one could get in or out. Everyone thought this was the end. But God knew better!

Three days later, early in the morning, the earth shook. An angel came and rolled the stone away from the tomb, and Jesus walked out. He was alive! God's plan was finished. And soon everyone would know!

—From Matthew 26:36—28:7

Jesus' Good News

When Jesus died and was buried in a tomb, his friends were very sad and afraid. They thought they would never see Jesus again. They thought they would never be happy again. They missed him so much.

Mary and some other women went to visit the place where Jesus was buried. They were very sad. But when they got there, Jesus wasn't in the tomb. An angel sat on a large stone and told the women some wonderful news. He told them that Jesus was alive! The women weren't sad any more. They were so happy that they ran to tell the good news to their friends.

Suddenly the women stopped because someone was standing in front of them. It was Jesus! The women could hardly believe that Jesus was really there. It seemed like a dream. But Jesus talked to them and said, "Tell my friends that I will meet them soon."

The women worshipped Jesus. They were happy that Jesus was alive. They were glad to see their friend.

—From Matthew 28:1-10

Breakfast by the Sea

Some of Jesus' closest friends were fishermen. One night, they went out in their boat to catch fish. They threw out their nets and waited all night long, but caught nothing.

When morning came, they were tired and hungry. They just wanted to go home. But someone called to them from the shore, "Haven't you caught any fish?"

"No," they yelled back, probably half asleep.

"Throw your nets on the other side of the boat. That's where the fish are!"

The fishermen threw their nets out again. Suddenly, their nets were so full of fish that they could hardly pull them in! Right away, Peter knew that the person calling to them must be Jesus. Peter was so happy to see Jesus that he jumped right out of the boat and swam to shore.

When the boat came in, Jesus was waiting with a fire and some bread. He asked his friends to bring some of the fish they caught. The fire was warm and the food was delicious. But the best thing about this breakfast was Jesus.

—*From John 21:1-14*

The First Christians

When Jesus went back to heaven, he had an important job for his friends. Jesus told them to go to everyone in the whole world and tell about him. Jesus wanted every person to know that he loves us, that he died for us, and that he's waiting for us in heaven.

Some of Jesus' friends traveled far away to teach about him. Others told about Jesus in the towns where they lived. Jesus' friends shared the good news in many different ways. A man named Peter talked about Jesus in front of huge crowds, so that everyone around him would hear about Jesus. A man named Paul took long trips on a ship. He talked to people in faraway places who didn't know about Jesus.

More and more people heard about Jesus and wanted to follow him. People gathered in homes and other places so they could pray and learn about Jesus together.

Families and friends all around the world spread the good news that Jesus is God's Son, and that He is alive!

—From Mark 16:15, Acts

Timothy Tells About Jesus

Timothy was a young boy. He had a kind mother named Eunice and a kind grandmother named Lois. Timothy's mother and grandmother loved and obeyed God. They taught him to love and obey God.

Timothy loved to hear his grandmother read from God's Book. She probably read stories about Moses and Samuel and David and many other helpers of God. Perhaps Timothy thought, "Maybe someday I can be a helper for God. Maybe I can be as brave as the people in God's Book."

Timothy grew older. He learned more and more about God's Book. He learned to read and study it by himself. One day a man named Paul came to the town where Timothy and Eunice and Lois lived. He taught Timothy and his mother and grandmother the good news about Jesus, God's Son. Paul said, "Timothy, you can tell others about Jesus too. Come and help me teach people in other countries how to live for God."

Timothy probably was very excited. "Paul wants me to go with him," thought Timothy. So Timothy and Paul traveled to many different cities and countries. Sometimes they walked, and sometimes they sailed on a ship. Timothy and Paul taught many people about Jesus. Timothy was a wonderful helper for Paul— and for God.

—From Acts 16:1-5; 2 Timothy 1:3-5